Step-by-Step
Beadwork

Michelle Powell

Heinemann Library
Chicago, Illinois

© 2002 Reed Educational & Professional Publishing
Published by Heinemann Library,
an imprint of Reed Educational & Professional Publishing,
Chicago, Illinois

Customer Service 888-454-2279

Visit our website at www.heinemannlibrary.com

Photographs by Charlotte de la Bédoyère,
Search Press Studios
Photographs and design copyright © Search Press Limited, 2002

Text copyright © Michelle Powell 2002
Designed by Search Press
Printed in Italy by L.E.G.O.

06 05 04 03 02
10 9 8 7 6 5 4 3 2 1

Library of Congress Cataloging-in-Publication Data

Powell, Michelle,
    Beadwork / Michelle Powell.
        p. cm. -- (Step-by-step)
    Summary: Introduces the history of beads and different tools
needed for beadwork, then provides step-by-step instructions for ten
beaded crafts, including a suncatcher, a key ring, and a puppet.
    Includes bibliographical references and index.
    ISBN 1-40340-696-0 (HC),   1-40340-715-0 (Pbk)
    1. Beadwork--Juvenile literature. [1. Beadwork. 2. Handicraft.]
I. Title. II. Step-by-step (Heinemann Library)
    TT860.P69 2002
    745. 58'2--dc21

                                        2001059392

Acknowledgments
The author and publishers are grateful to the following for
permission to reproduce copyright material:
Bridgeman Art Library, page 5.

Photographs: Search Press Studios

Every effort has been made to contact copyright holders of any
material reproduced in this book. Any omissions will be rectified in
subsequent printings if notice is given to the publisher.

This book is for Zac.

Some words are shown in bold, **like this.**
You can find out what they mean by
looking in the glossary.

When this sign is used in the
book, it means that adult
supervision is needed.

REMEMBER!
Ask an adult to help you
when you see this sign.

Contents

Introduction

Beads have been used for thousands of years in many different countries around the world. The earliest beads were found in the tombs of ancient Egyptians. Beads were used to make jewelry and they were also used as money. It became popular for people to carry their money beads on a string around their necks to keep the beads safe. It also showed their wealth and importance.

Certain types of beads also showed a person's religious or superstitious beliefs. The word bead came from the Old English word *bede*, meaning prayer. People of many religions carried strings of beads. Each bead represented a prayer or psalm. Some people carried a talisman — a carved stone or other small object. They believed that it would ward off evil spirits.

Beads are now more normally used to make attractive jewelry and in craft projects like the ones in this book.

There are many different types of beads available. Some are made from beautiful gemstones dug from the ground such as **turquoise**. Amber beads are made from tree resins that have hardened in the ground for thousands of years. Precious metals such as gold and silver are also made into beads. Pearls are beads made in an oyster shell. This happens when a tiny grain of sand gets into the shell. The oyster surrounds it with a special substance to make it smooth.

Many beads are made from glass. They are blown into shape or cut by highly skilled craftspeople. Wood and clay are also popular materials used to make beads. Plastic beads are made in lots of shapes and colors.

This book shows you how to make many projects using beads and beading techniques. There are patterns at the end of the book to help you, and page 28 shows you how to **transfer** them onto your projects. You can make some of the beads yourself from air-drying clay, felt, or **high-density foam.** Other projects use store-bought beads such as tiny seed beads, plastic pony beads, and **polystyrene** balls.

*Opposite These beads and amulets were found in the tombs of ancient Egyptian **pharaohs.** They are made from faience—a type of glazed pottery—gold, and semiprecious stones. Amulets were believed to protect the wearer from evil. The turquoise beads with jackal and hawk heads are two of the sons of the god Horus. They were put in a tomb to protect the mummy.*

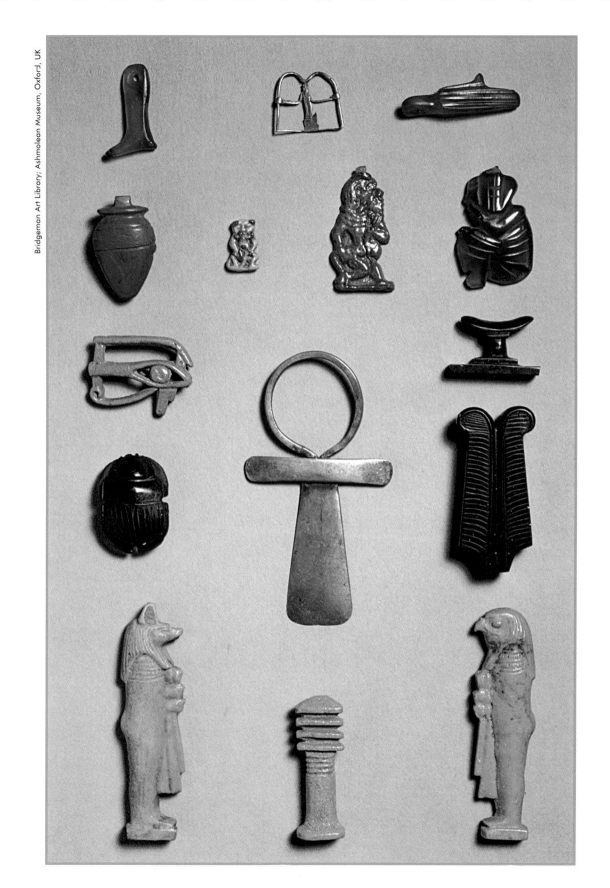

Materials

The items pictured here are the basic tools and equipment you will need to complete the projects featured in this book. You will also need cardboard to make **templates**. Some of the projects involve making your own beads. Others use store-bought beads. Beads can be made from a number of different things that you may have at home. Remember that whenever you use paints, glue, or clay, you should cover your working area with newspaper or scrap paper.

You can make beads from **high-density foam**. Store-bought beads include *pony beads*, *seed beads*, *bugle beads* and *faceted beads*. *Sequins* are used to decorate projects. A *split ring* is used to make the Gecko Key Ring on pages 20–21. A *bell* decorates the Indian Wall Hanging. *Suction cups* attach projects to windows.

Polystyrene balls and blocks are used to make large beads.

Drinking straws are used to make beads.

Cotton balls are used to stuff bead shapes.

A *clay cutting tool* is used to shape the clay beads.

A *pipe cleaner* is used to thread beads onto.

A *ruler* is used to measure and draw straight lines.

Wooden dowels are used for making puppets and beaded curtains.

You can make beads from colored *felt*. *Fabric* can be cut into fringes and beaded.

Newspaper and a *rolling pin* are used to roll the *clay* in bead making. A *chopping board* is useful when cutting materials.

A small *plant pot*, *wire*, *gravel*, **oasis,** and a *knife* are used to make the Bonsai Tree. Oasis is a type of foam used to make flower arrangements. Ask an adult to help you cut it.

A *pencil*, *tracing paper*, and **carbon paper** are used for transferring the patterns from the back of the book. You might need to go over your designs with a *felt tip pen*.

Multipurpose glue and *fabric glue* are used to stick beads, felt, and sequins in place. Brown *flower tape* is used to wrap wire for the Bonsai Tree. *Masking tape* is used when transferring a design.

A *potato chip can* is used as the base for the Southwestern Shaker.

Kebab sticks are used for piercing holes, and for hanging strings of beads.

Water-based *acrylic paints* or *poster paints* and a small *paint brush* are used for the projects in this book.

Scissors are used to cut string, felt and foam. *Old scissors* are useful for cutting thin wire. *Pinking scissors* are used to cut felt to make patterns on some beads.

String and *elastic thread* are used to thread your beads. *Darning needles* and other *large needles* such as **bodkins** are useful for threading and for piercing holes. The *wooden picture frame* is to decorate with beads. *Toothpicks* are used to position tiny beads.

Bonsai Tree

In Japan, the art of growing tiny trees in shallow pots is called Bonsai. You can make beaded Bonsai trees by using sequins, flower beads, and wire. Fix the trees in some **oasis** and put them in small pots on your windowsill. You could make a spring tree covered in pink blossoms, or use leaf beads or sequins in oranges, browns, and reds for an autumn tree.

YOU WILL NEED

30 pieces of wire, 9in. (23cm) long
Some extra wire
Flower beads • Leaf sequins
Oasis • Brown flower tape
Small plant pot • Chopping board
Old scissors • Knife • Ruler
Fine gravel • Multipurpose glue

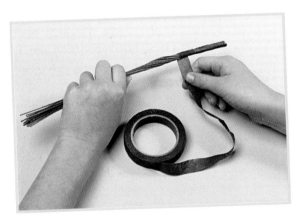

1 Using old scissors, cut thirty pieces of wire, 9in. (23cm) long. Twist the pieces together until you reach the middle. Wrap brown flower tape around the twist. This will be the tree trunk.

2 Split the bunch of wires into seven groups. Each group will make a branch of the tree. Twist the wires in each branch together to about half way along the branch.

(!) Ask an adult to help you to cut the wire.

3 Divide each branch into two smaller branches. Twist the wires of the smaller branches together for a few inches. Leave wires sticking out in a v shape at the end of each branch to look like twigs.

4

Ask an adult to help you to cut fourteen 2in. (5cm) lengths of wire, using old scissors. Add them to the v shapes at the ends of your branches. Twist them onto each side of the v to thicken your twigs.

5

Take a flower bead and push a wire twig through the hole. Push the bead ½in. (1cm) down the twig. Bend back the end of the wire toward the center of the flower. Now push a leaf sequin ½in. (1cm) down another twig. Bend the wire over the top of the leaf and tuck it in around the back. Decorate the whole tree with flowers and leaves.

6

Using a knife and a chopping board, carefully cut oasis to fit your pot and push it in. Push in your bonsai tree. Cover the top of the oasis with multipurpose glue, and sprinkle on gravel.

Ask an adult to help you to cut the oasis.

FURTHER IDEAS

Make a bonsai garden, or cut a bird from cardboard and put it in a bonsai tree for Christmas.

Indian Wall Hanging

Traditional Indian clothes are made from bright fabrics in beautiful colors. This wall hanging is like an Indian decoration with its bright colors and shiny sequins. The stuffed felt beads are in the shape of birds, which often appear in Indian art and crafts. The small beads are rolled from strips of felt and decorated with felt in different colors. Straws are used to make holes through the beads so that they are easier to string together.

1 **Transfer** the bird design on page 29 onto cardboard. Cut out the shapes and draw around them on felt, using a felt tip pen. Cut out two body shapes (front and back) and two wings for each bird. The wings should be in a different color than the body.

2 Put a line of fabric glue around the edge of one back body piece. Lay a straw on the felt, and put part of a cotton ball on top.

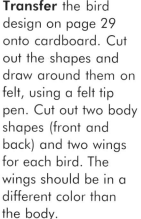

3 Push a front body piece onto the glue so that the two halves of the bird stick together. Repeat steps 1–3 for four more birds.

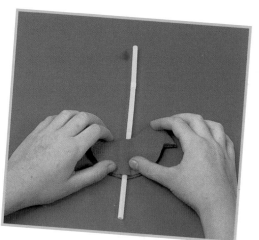

4

Glue different colored wings onto each bird. Glue on small triangles of yellow felt for beaks. Glue on pieces of sequin for decoration. Cut off the excess straw close to the felt.

5

Cut thirteen strips of felt, 3¼in. (8cm) long and ½in. (1cm) wide. Cover one side of each strip with fabric glue and roll each strip around a straw to make felt beads. Let them dry and then cut off the excess straw close to the felt.

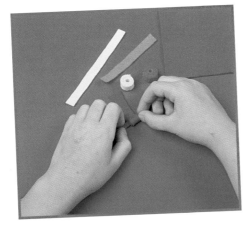

6

Use pinking scissors to cut strips of felt 2in. (5cm) long and ¼in. (5mm) wide. Glue the strips around the felt beads for decoration. Tie a bell onto a 23½in. (60cm) piece of string. Push the string through the straws inside two felt beads. Next, thread a bird onto the string in the same way. Then add two more felt beads. Continue until all the birds are on the string. Add three beads at the top.

FURTHER IDEAS

Design your own Indian wall hanging using an elephant shape instead of a bird.

Egyptian Picture Frame

King Tutankhamen was a famous Egyptian **pharaoh.** After he died, a beautiful mask was made of his face and buried with him in his tomb. More than three thousand years later, **archaeologists** discovered this mask and many other buried treasures. This picture frame uses small seed beads and long, straight bugle beads glued onto a wooden frame in a **mosaic** style to create the look of King Tutankhamen's beautiful mask.

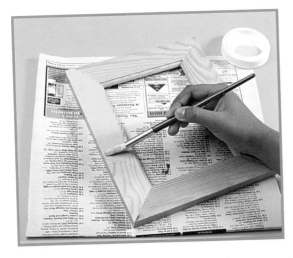

1 Paint the picture frame a light color, using acrylic poster paint. Let it dry.

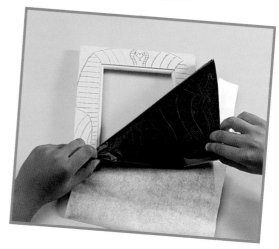

2 **Transfer** the design on page 29 onto the frame.

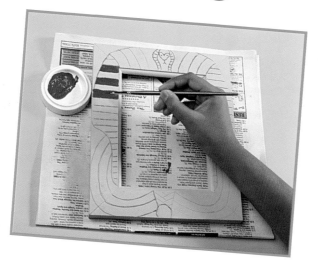

3 Paint stripes of color on the frame as shown. Continue painting the design, leaving blank areas for beads between the painted stripes.

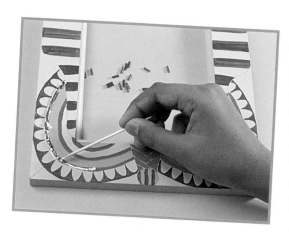

Paint the other areas of the design as shown and let them dry. Put a line of glue on the design. Use a toothpick with a little glue on the end to pick up the long colored bugle beads. Position the beads along the glued line.

Squeeze a thin layer of glue onto the unpainted semicircles at the bottom of the frame. Arrange the long gold beads, using the toothpick as before. Add glue to the unpainted striped areas and sprinkle on gold seed beads.

6 Press down on the gold seed beads. Sprinkle on more to fill any gaps and let the frame dry.

FURTHER IDEAS

Design your own frame, and put in a picture inspired by the ancient Egyptians.

Fish Pencil Toppers

Decorate your pencils and pens by making beaded fish toppers. The fish are made from a **polystyrene** ball, and sequins are used to look like the fish's scales. Small plastic faceted beads are used to make the fins and tail. Faceted beads are cut to have many flat faces or facets, like diamonds. They will give a shimmery feel to your fish. You could find some pictures of fish to copy, or just use your imagination to create colorful fishy friends.

YOU WILL NEED

Pencil to decorate
Sequins • Beads
Thin wire • Multipurpose glue
1½in. (4cm) polystyrene balls
Scissors • Old scissors
Darning needle
Ruler

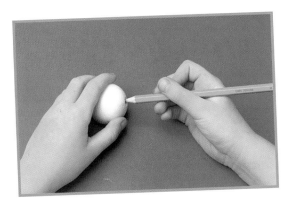

1 Use the pencil to make a hole in the polystyrene ball.

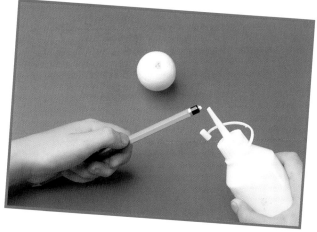

2 Glue the ball to the top of the pencil using multipurpose glue. Let it dry.

3 Starting at the pencil hole, glue a line of sequins onto the ball. Cover half of the ball with colored sequins in the same way, and the other half with clear sequins. The clear sequins will make the fish's face. Let it dry.

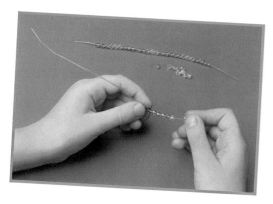

4

Use old scissors to cut two pieces of 7in. (18cm) wire. Thread twenty-five beads on one wire for the tail and twenty-five on the other for the fin. Bend the beaded wires into tail and fin shapes like those shown on page 31.

Ask an adult to help you to cut the wire.

5

Make two holes in the ball with the darning needle where you want to add the fin. Put a little glue on each hole. Take the beaded fin and push one end of it into each hole. Do the same for the tail.

Ask an adult to help you to use the darning needle.

6

Place a little glue on either side of the face for the eyes and in the center for the mouth. Push a black faceted bead onto the glue for the eyes, and a clear faceted bead for the mouth.

FURTHER IDEAS
Make beaded fish without the hole for a pencil. Attach magnets to the side to make refrigerator magnets.

African Beaded Curtain

The shapes and colors of this beaded curtain are taken from designs used to decorate African pottery. The leaves and curling vines look like the hanging canopy found in African forests. The beads are made from **high-density foam** shapes and drinking straws. Hang the curtain in the doorway of your bedroom to give it an African theme.

YOU WILL NEED
High-density foam
Scissors • **Bodkin**
Acrylic poster paint • Paint brush
Drinking straws • String • Pencil
Masking tape • Cardboard
Tracing paper • **Carbon paper**
Wooden dowel cut to the width
of your doorway

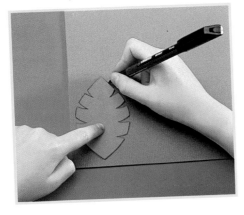

1 **Transfer** the patterns from page 30 on to cardboard. Cut out leaf, triangle, star, zigzag, and diamond **templates.** Draw around the templates on foam of several different colors.

2 Cut out eleven of each shape from the different colored foam. Cut out eleven foam strips. Each should be 11¾ x ¾in. (30 x 2cm) long.

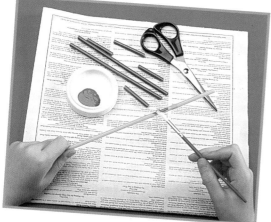

3 Paint the straws different colors and cut them into various different lengths.

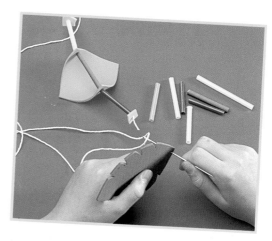

4 Cut seven pieces of string. Each should be 6½ft. (2m) long. Thread one end of a shape onto a string. Thread on a short piece of colored straw, then thread on the other end of the shape. Thread a piece of straw in between each shape. Continue threading the shapes in this way.

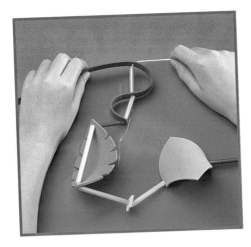

5 To thread the strips, make a small mark on each strip every 2¼in. (6cm). Starting at one end, thread the needle and string through the strip, then through a short piece of straw, then again through the strip. Repeat to the end of the strip.

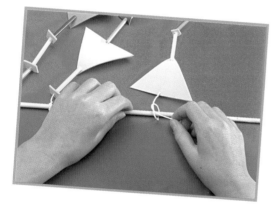

6 Thread shapes and straws onto all of the strings. Tie the end of each string onto the dowel. The curtain is now ready to put up in your doorway.

Ask an adult to cut the dowel to the right length, and to hang the finished curtain for you.

FURTHER IDEAS
Decorate a foam band and put it around your head to make an African headdress.

Southwestern Shaker

People in the southwest often made clothes and bags with a beaded tassel trim. They cut animal hide into strips and threaded it with beads for decoration. This shaker is made in a similar way, using felt cut into tassels with pony beads threaded on to make a design. The felt is wrapped around a can filled with more beads so that you can make music.

1 Cut a piece of fabric large enough to fit around the potato chip can. Cover the can with multipurpose glue and leave it until it is almost dry. Glue on the fabric.

2 Cut two strips of felt: one 2¾in. (7cm) wide and the second 7in. (18cm) wide. Both must be long enough to go around the can. Draw lines ½in. (1cm) apart on the strips. Use the lines as a guide and cut fringes ¾in. (2cm) from the top, as shown.

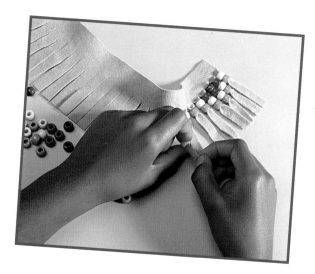

 3 Make a pattern by threading different colored pony beads onto the fringe of the narrower strip, as shown. Then decorate the other fringes in the same way.

4

Glue the strip with the long fringe around the can so that the tassels hang to the bottom of the can. Glue the short fringe around the can near the top.

5

Put any leftover beads into the can to make the shaker noise.

6

Draw around the lid and cut out a circle of felt. Glue it onto the lid. Add a blue trim. **Transfer** the star and circle patterns on page 29 onto felt and cut them out. Stick the star onto the lid. Thread some decorative beads onto two 4in. (10cm) pieces of string. Snip a tiny hole in the middle of the circle. Push the ends of the strings through the hole and glue the circle on top of the star.

FURTHER IDEAS
Make a fringed drum from a plastic margarine tub to go with your shaker.

Gecko Key Ring

Geckos are lizards that live in warm countries. Their feet stick to smooth surfaces so that they can run up walls and even across ceilings! These gecko key rings are made by threading colored pony beads onto string to form the shape of the gecko. This technique is ideal for making reptiles like snakes, frogs, or turtles, because the beads look like the patterns on scaly skin.

YOU WILL NEED

Eighty-five different colored pony beads
Split ring
String
Scissors

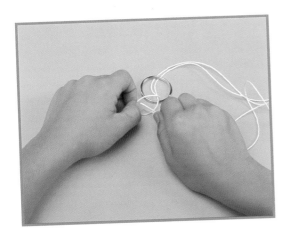

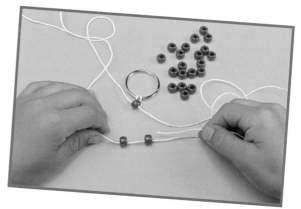

1 Cut 39in. (1m) of string. Fold it in half and loop it through the split ring. Push the two ends of the string through the loop and pull tight.

2 Look at the pattern on page 31. Thread one bead onto one of the strings, then push the other string through the bead in the opposite direction. Push the bead right up to the ring. Next, thread two beads onto one string and thread the other string through in the opposite direction. Push both beads tight against the first bead.

3

Continue following the pattern to make the gecko's head. Push the beads tight against each other after threading each row. To make the first leg, thread three dark and three light colored beads onto one string. Bring the string around and thread it back through the dark beads.

4

Make the second leg on the string on the other side. Now continue with the body, following the pattern on page 31. Pull the strings tight after threading on each row of beads.

5

Make the gecko's back legs in the same way as the front legs. Next, thread two beads onto the string on one side. Then thread the other string through the beads in the opposite direction. Continue following the pattern in the same way to make the tail.

6

Tie off the strings together at the end of the tail. Now thread three more beads onto each remaining length of string for decoration. Knot and cut off both strings.

FURTHER IDEAS

Make zipper pulls or a mobile with your beaded creatures, or use glow in the dark beads to make aliens or ghosts!

Rainbow Sun Catcher

This sun catcher's pattern is in the shape of a traditional stained-glass window. For this sun catcher, you need pony beads that are colored but **transparent**, so that the light will shine through them, as well as some **opaque** beads. The beads are threaded onto strings so that when they are hung together, they will form a picture of the sun rising, a rainbow, and a moonlit sky all in a window frame. Stick your sun catcher to your window and wait for some sunshine to bring it to life!

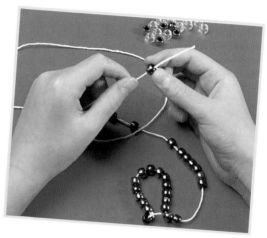

1 Cut twenty-four pieces of string. Each should be 20in. (50cm) long. Tie one black pony bead to one end of twenty-three of the pieces. Tie an opaque metallic bead to the end of the twenty-fourth string. Pull the knots tight.

2 Look at the pattern on page 31. Thread opaque metallic beads onto the first string. Then add nineteen clear beads onto the same string. Thread the last clear bead onto the string.

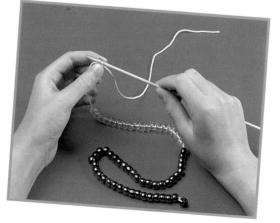

3 Insert the pointed end of the kebab stick into the last clear bead on the string. Tie the end of the string around the kebab stick and cut it off close to the stick.

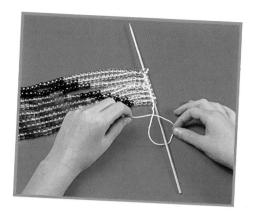

4

Follow the pattern and continue to thread the beads onto the string, one column at a time. Push the kebab stick through each final bead and tie the string around the kebab stick as shown.

5

Continue following the pattern, tying off the ends and cutting off the excess string.

6

Hook three suction cups onto the kebab stick. Now the sun catcher is ready to be attached to your window.

FURTHER IDEAS

Add bells to the bottom of the sun catcher. Hang it up outside to make a wind chime.

Astronaut Puppet

This project uses **polystyrene** balls as huge beads strung together to make an astronaut puppet. You will need polystyrene balls in the following shapes and sizes: two 3¼in. (8cm) egg shapes for the hands, two 4in. (10cm) egg shapes for the feet, one 3½in. (9cm) ball for the head, one 4¼in. (11cm) ball for the body, two 2¼in. (6cm) balls for the shoulders, four 3¼in. (8cm) balls for the legs, and four 2¾in. (7cm) balls for the arms and legs.

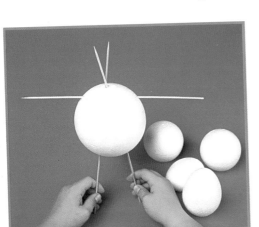

1 Use a kebab stick to push a hole straight through the middle of all of the polystyrene balls except the body. Make three holes in the body as shown, and then pull out the kebab sticks.

> **(!)** Ask an adult to help you to make holes with the kebab sticks.

2 Paint two of the egg shapes as gloves and the other two as space boots. Paint the details of the face and helmet and the body. Paint the polystyrene block. This will be the astronaut's oxygen tank.

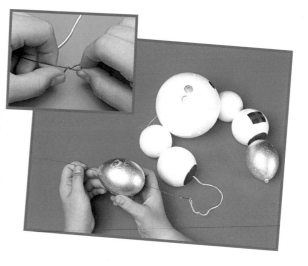

Twist a long piece of wire into a needle shape, as shown. Thread elastic thread through the "eye" of the needle and tie a large knot at the end. Slide on a small bead, a glove, two arm beads, the body, two more arm beads, the other glove, and another clear plastic bead. Tie another large knot in the elastic thread.

Use the wire needle to thread another piece of elastic thread through a small bead, a boot, and three leg beads. Push the needle up through one of the body holes and down through the second hole. Thread on three more leg beads, a boot, and another clear plastic bead. Tie a knot.

4

5 Thread a piece of elastic thread down through the head bead and tie it to the loop left by the legs. Glue the oxygen tank to the body with multipurpose glue. Thread some clear beads onto a pipe cleaner, and push one end in the helmet and the other end in the oxygen tank.

6 Make four small wire hooks. Stick them into the knees and hands. Tie on four lengths of string 29½in. (75cm) long. Tie the other ends to the two pieces of wooden dowel tied in a cross shape. Put another wire hook in the head, and use string to attach it to the center of the dowel cross.

FURTHER IDEAS
Thread painted polystyrene balls onto string and hang them up to make a planet mobile.

Aztec Game

The **Aztecs** lived in Mexico around five hundred years ago. They made amazing art and crafts. They carved the shapes of faces and animals into tall wooden poles. This game is based on Aztec sculptures. The playing pieces are large clay beads in the shapes of birds and faces. You need fourteen birds and fourteen faces to play **three-dimensional** tic-tac-toe.

YOU WILL NEED
Air-drying clay
Rolling pin • Clay cutting tool
Ruler • Drinking straw
Acrylic poster paint • Paint brush
Nine pieces of thin wooden dowel
6in. (15cm) long
Block of **polystyrene** 6¼in. (16cm) square
Multipurpose glue • Felt, two different colors
Tracing paper • **Carbon paper**
Cardboard • Scissors • Pencil
Masking tape

1 **Transfer** the tail, feet, and wing patterns on page 30 onto cardboard and cut them out to make **templates.**

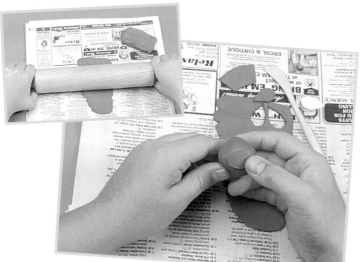

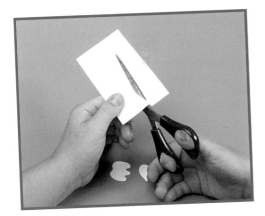

2 Using your hands, roll twenty-eight balls of clay the size of a walnut. Use the straw to make a hole through the middle of each ball.

3 Roll out a piece of clay about ⅛ in. (4mm) thick and use the templates to cut out wing, feet, and tail shapes for the birds. Stick these to fourteen of the clay beads.

 4

Roll tiny clay balls for the eyes. Press them onto the clay beads, using a little water to help them stick. Use a clay cutting tool to indent the eyeballs and make grooves in the wings and tails. Let them dry.

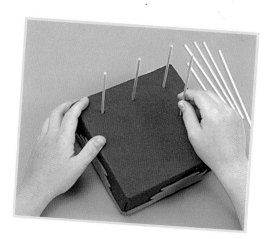

5

Paint the fourteen bird beads and let them dry. Now make fourteen Aztec face beads using the face pattern on page 30. Paint them, too.

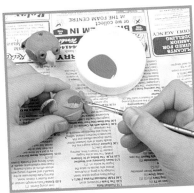

6

Cover the square of polystyrene with felt. Use the pattern on page 30 to make a felt decoration for each side. Push the pieces of dowel into the square in evenly spaced rows of three. Now you can play three-dimensional tic-tac-toe with the birds and face beads—any straight line of three beads wins!

FURTHER IDEAS

Make a checker board from cardboard and use your beads to play checkers.

Transferring Patterns

You can trace the patterns on these pages straight from the book (step 1). You can make them larger or smaller on a photocopier if you wish, and then follow steps 2–4 to **transfer** them onto your project.

 Ask an adult to help you enlarge the patterns on a photocopier.

1 Place a piece of tracing paper over the pattern and tape it down with small pieces of masking tape. Trace around the outlines using a soft pencil. Or, photocopy the design.

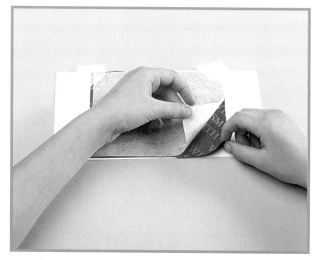

2 Place the tracing paper or photocopy on the surface of the project and tape it at the top. Slide the **carbon paper** face down between the tracing paper and the project. Tape it at the bottom.

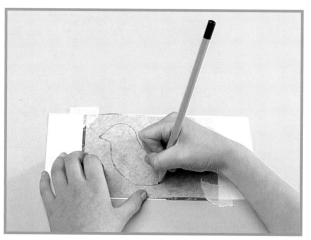

3 Trace over the outlines with the pencil, pressing down firmly.

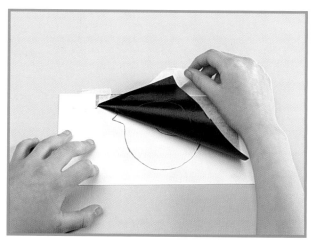

4 Remove the tracing paper and the carbon paper to reveal the design.

Patterns

Patterns for the Indian
Wall Hanging featured
on pages 10–11

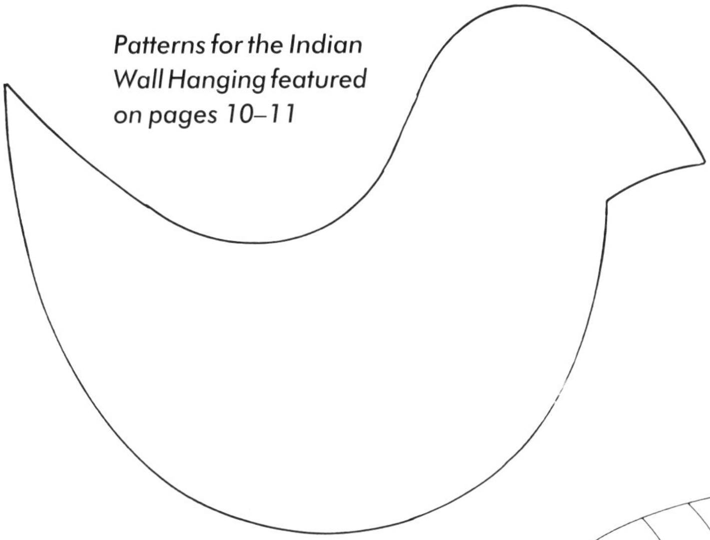

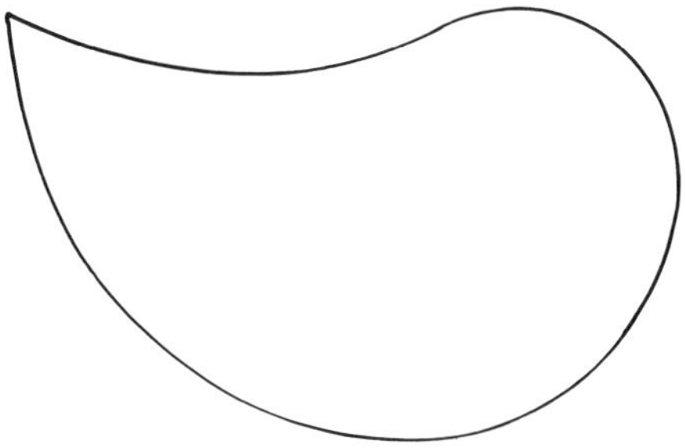

Patterns for the
Southwestern
Shaker featured on pages 18–19

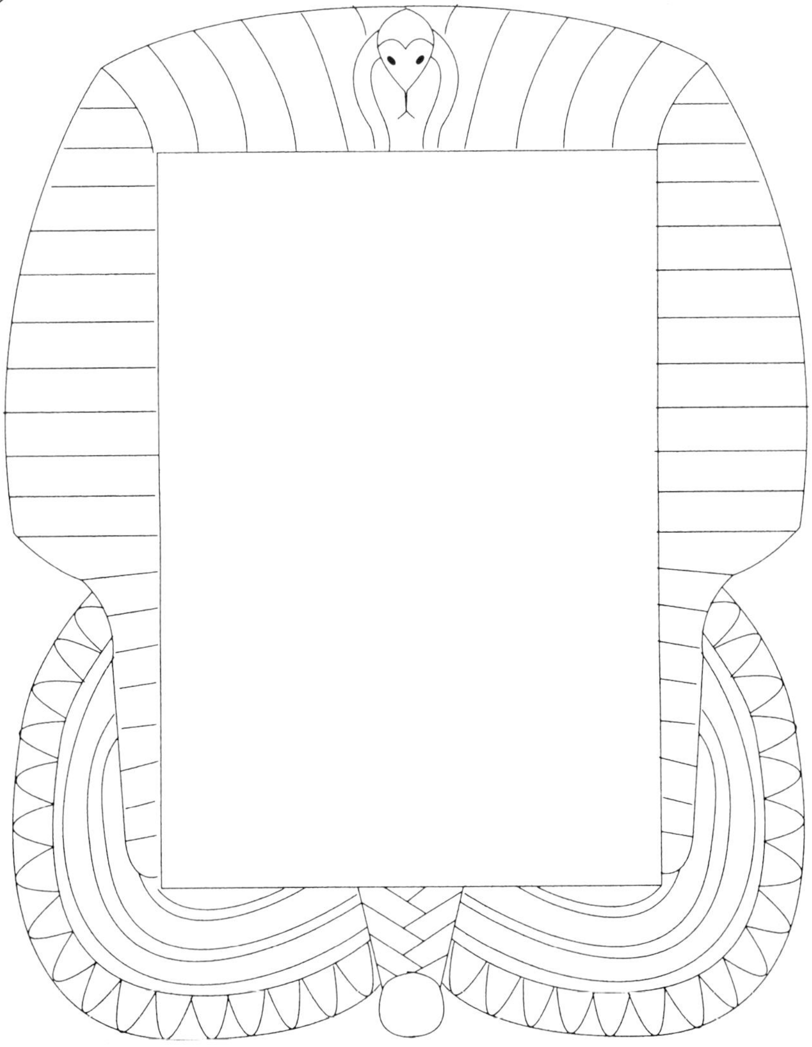

Pattern for the Egyptian
Picture Frame featured on
pages 12–13

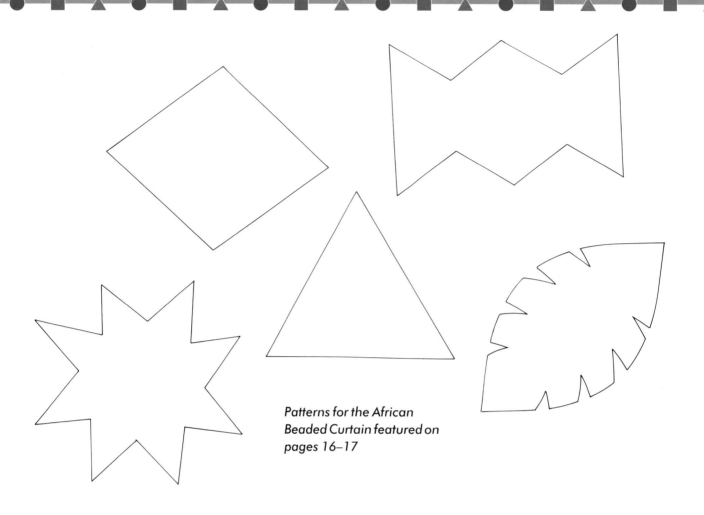

Patterns for the African Beaded Curtain featured on pages 16–17

Patterns for the **Aztec** Game featured on pages 26–27.
Top left to right: tail, feet, wing, and face patterns.
Bottom: felt decoration for the base.

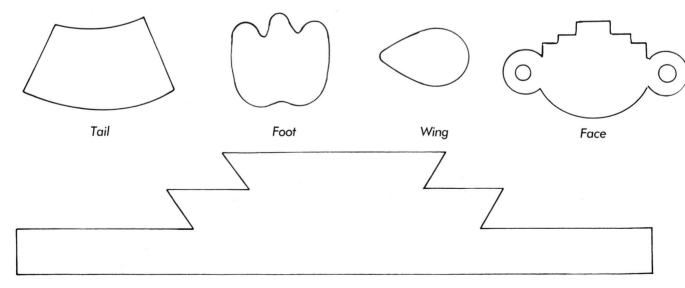

Tail   Foot   Wing   Face

Decoration for base

Pattern for the Rainbow Sun Catcher featured on pages 22–23

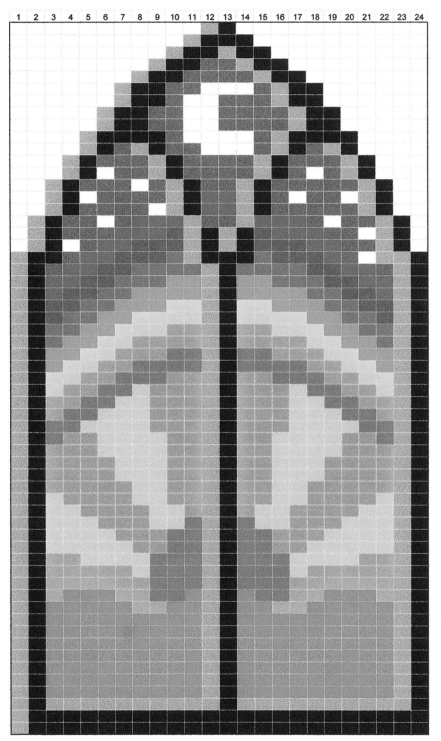

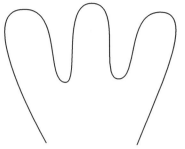

Patterns for the Fish Pencil Toppers featured on pages 14–15

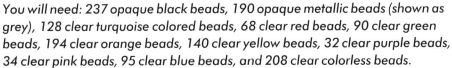
You will need: 237 opaque black beads, 190 opaque metallic beads (shown as grey), 128 clear turquoise colored beads, 68 clear red beads, 90 clear green beads, 194 clear orange beads, 140 clear yellow beads, 32 clear purple beads, 34 clear pink beads, 95 clear blue beads, and 208 clear colorless beads.

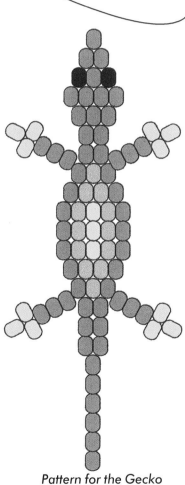

Pattern for the Gecko Key Ring featured on pages 20–21

Glossary

Archaeologist person who digs up and studies things left behind from past times

Aztec people who lived in the fifteenth and early sixteenth centuries in what is now central and southern Mexico

Bodkin needle with a very large eye

Carbon paper paper with a dark coating that is placed between two pieces of plain paper so that pencil marks on the top piece of paper go through to the second piece

High-density foam special kind of foam used in arts and crafts that is sold at craft stores

Kebab stick pointed wooden stick used to hold meat and vegetables for grilling

Mosaic picture or image made up of small colored pieces of tile or glass

Oasis a type of foam used to hold flower arrangements

Opaque something that does not allow light to show through

Pharaoh ancient Egyptian king

Polystyrene stiff, plastic foam often used for cups for hot liquids such as coffee and hot chocolate

Template pattern or guide for copying an image once or many times

Three-dimensional seeming to have width, height, and depth; appearing real and solid

Transfer to move something from one place to another

Transparent see-through

Turquoise greenish-blue stone found frequently in the southwestern United States and often used in jewelry

More Books to Read

Ackerman, Janice S. *Craft Cord Corral: Bead Stringing Projects for Everyone.* Liberty, Utah : Eagles View Publishing, 1995.

Korach, Alice. *Bead Art.* Waukesha, Wis. : Kalmach Publishing Company, 1998.

White, Mary. *How to Do Bead Work.* Magnolia, Mass. : Peter Smith Publishing, Inc., 1990.

Index